For Sinead and Shane

From the Pirate and Mary!

Binnion Road

Des Kavanagh

*For Mary, Ronan, Conal,
and in memory of Rory.*

Books of *taste*, Created with *passion*, In the heart of *Connemara*.

www.artisanhouse.ie

The thing about writing is that if you have the impulse, you will find the time.

Seamus Heaney
RTÉ, December 1995.

Foreword
Seamus Deane

Des Kavanagh's poems are full of the names of
people and places he knows or has known well. The people he
commemorates in them – for many of these poems are salutes
to the dead – are observed with such a calm and steady gaze
that it takes the reader one, maybe two beats to catch the
counter-current of feeling that at times makes the poems
rock uneasily at anchor. Names are great familiarisers and
Kavanagh's Ireland is a close and familiar place. But it also
bears within it the ache of absence, not just for specific people,
but for the world they inhabited, a world that made them and
that they also made. Kavanagh's ancestral Inishowen in
Donegal, his family, in its old and new generations, often
provide the pivot that turns him to the past, although it also
allows for glimpses of the future, through children and
grandchildren. Kierkegaards's famous remark, now almost a
proverb, often becomes live again in the circuits of such poetry:
'Life can only be understood backwards but it must
be lived forwards.'

The particular sway and movement of many of these poems
can be caught by listening carefully to their patterns
of sound. The rhythms are regular, placid even. But the
accented features, the regular weak and strong, strong and weak
shadings, are skilfully melded with a colloquial ease of speech
that relaxes the poems, once the iambic rhythm section is
subdued. Kavanagh has also learned how to bring a poem up
short, in a single full-stopped word, as in 'Love Observed',
which closes with
'Together.
Apart.'

That to some degree explains for me the ache, the sense of loss that can arise from the listed place names of the verse, like the wisp of a clarinet solo, the sigh of a double bass, amid more ordinary, daily sounds.

In one of his finest poems, 'Far and Near', he finds
> 'I am both far and near
> alienated in a place
> I thought familiar',

the word 'alienated' keeps part of the sound of 'Leenan', four lines earlier. It is a subtle effect, the assonance between words that enact the contrast that the poem explores. That is also audible in the stacked single-word, single-line Gaelic place names of 'Western Distributor Road', where the title squats on the traditional ground and names, a reminder how effective a title can be as an active part of the poem.

The reader has to be nimble as a spider in a web in tracking these poems through the air, for they expand or contract, often quite suddenly, as they move from their regular accented patterns to the syllabic sheen of a person's or place's well-known name. This can make a poem flex briefly like a muscle from plain statement to an ache of memory, a moment of pathos.

Des Kavanagh has long been known for his father's role in the recording of Charles McGlinchey's memoir *The Last of the Name* (1986). It appealed to many readers because of its peculiarly sweet combination of nostalgia and majesty, the majesty of an individual deriving from a sense of communal pride that, before it begins to fade, finds its last flare in him. Brian Friel skilfully edited the original continuous manuscript and broke it into chapters. He also wrote a remarkable Introduction.

Kavanagh's sense of communal pride is jokingly displayed in the acrostic poem 'Tribal Naming' but more sombrely in others, such as 'Visitors', where McGlinchey himself appears as his stories and memories are transmitted into history by the poet's father. That is the kind of transitional moment, oral to written culture, which we feel is being sought in several poems here. In 'The King's Instructions', dedicated to McGlinchey, that composite of the quotidian with the marvellous, comic and haunting, is exemplified. The loss of that earlier richness is one of the sources of the quiet lamentation we occasionally hear. We can sense too in these poems the charismatic presence of Seamus Heaney, a close friend of Kavanagh's since secondary school days (at St. Columb's in Derry). There is a poem 'After Seamus Heaney' ('Had I Not Been Awake I Would Have Missed it'). Heaney's influence is palpable throughout, contemplative, charged, observant. It's clearly felt in 'Heirloom', about an egg-timer, especially at the end of the first verse:

> 'A little rush of streaming sand
> let time fall.'

But it is perhaps in the elegy to his mother in her widowhood, 'Keeping On', that he strikes that Heaney-esque end-note more clearly, as she finally is 'soothed by the pull and catch of stitch.'

Kavanagh has absorbed the gift of deepening the emotional reach
of a poem in its concluding line and also, in that single stroke,
making the title itself an accelerant for the final blaze. It takes a
sure timing to achieve this; one stress too many, one syllable too
few and the effect may be lost, may become schmaltzy or cute.
'Milk Trail' is one lovely example of how to avoid this:

> 'trailing milk all the way home'

with its familiarising names of people, Matt Wilson and Hugh
McCarron enhancing the memory, all the more piercing for the
closeness they bring and then the distance that opens in the final
word, 'home'. In 'Uplift', which refers both to the shouldering of
the coffin of a traditional musician and to the effect of his music
on his audience, the finale is suitably grand and melancholy, as
above Achill sound the mist comes down,

> 'a great blind drawn across
> the horizon.'

On the occasion of his parents visiting him for the first time
when he is a boarder at St. Columb's, the characteristic shift
of the last lines weaves the colloquial accent of Donegal with
the lightly disturbed iambic measure; as his parents depart,
he suddenly sees them closer to one another than they have
ever been;

> 'closer than I had ever seen them
> Head away for home down Bishop Street.'

The name of the street suddenly becomes an intimacy of feeling.
Here we have poetry. Des Kavanagh has achieved for himself
his own music and we are the better, the richer, for being able
to hear it.

Behind The Windows This Is Working

after Billy Collins

The poets are at their windows
finding a compass to where
no one's been before.
Out of sight of passing joggers
jabbering children, star-struck lovers
they will light wicks of radiance.
And sail alone around rooms, with
jittery pens in search of revelation
for new energies and rhythms.
Assemble poem-life out of wonder.
Be trusted to find its way.

Visitors

I

I can still hear those women talking at our table, parcelling
knitted clothes for grandchildren to emigrant daughters.
My mother hoarded string, sealing wax, bundles of used
brown paper, wrote labels to addresses exotic in my ear:
Spalding Lincs. Leamington Spa. Boston Mass. Chorley Lancs.
and best of all *Sauchiehall Street Glasgow.* Was that near
Parkhead? I raced for the mail bus
that left at four; the post mistress might be cross if you
were late.

II

Uncle Jim always late, arrived like a secret at bedtime.
We'd draw on his drinker's breath when he went on
about local scandal, neighbours' rows, new romances
or houses built with hardware he supplied: *building blocks,
Wavin pipes, knobs for doors, the best of slates* – and loads of
credit out.
Once around midnight, he piled coal on the fire.
We'd hope he'd never leave.

III

The fire was lit when Charlie McGlinchey called
to share his folklore with my father.
It was to the hearth he spoke, in a flat voice
in country kitchens when neighbours gathered.
Parish history tumbled out: *the homes, the land,*
cures and spells, The Fair at Pollan, Colonel McNeil,
The Waterloo Priest. My father transcribed
his spoken words to history written.

Western Distributor Road

I walk the dog
along the vast new space
a settled-down mid-morning feel pervades
where mothers rushed with fresh-faced girls
and close-cropped boys in jeeps.
Empty streets
recall place names of old Rahoon
Tor Buí
Bin Bann
Drom Oir
Carrigeen.
Before the builders came
farmers toiled and walked this land
gorse grew where families settle now.
It's like a whole new town.
Never ending twin-like rows
of silent curtained homes.
Past mortgaged dreams
I walk the dog.

St. Jude's

In our isolation unit for the infected,
men murmur and sigh in their sleep.
Confined, drip-fed, obedient. A nurse
in white shoes passes with a night-light.

Minutes drag like winters.
A farmer shouts, 'Get that calf to the vet!'
He has brown beads on his locker
and a card From Your Dear Wife.

A full moon brightens the window
as we are freighted through the night.
Car noise, talk from the apparently well
drift towards us from hushed streets.

Milk Trail

On winter evenings
I'd walk to McCarron's farm
up past the graveyard
with its rusting gates
along the winding lane,
the stone-lined well.

Inside the door I stood obedient
while the milk poured
from white enamelled jugs
kept cool on the stone floor.
Old Matt Wilson and Hugh McCarron
bent towards the fire
told stories of banshee wails
a one-eyed lady at the well
or men from the parish recently deceased
seen selling fish at night
at others' graves.

With two quart cans
I'd head down the dark lane,
flee past the well,
creaking gates
and gravestones that glistened
trailing milk all the way home.

Retail Therapy

Rumour, before I knew the meaning
drifted over the bar's partition
in the murmured talk of men drinking.
Dried ling curled on a shelf
where bacon hung on hooks
and herring barrels stood open.
There, a frail figure busy
in her lifetime's counter space
organised, rearranged, parcelled
neat-bagged goods scooped from sacks
and tea chests – works of art
hand-made and handed over.
She weighed out snuff with instinct
a poke of powder balanced
against a tiny brass weight.
We willed her on, in silence,
as if the balance was with us.
Soon, no one's lost for words.
I saw her listen as they went on
without saying everything, in the give
and take of practised conversation.

Moville

I am deep-rooted in these lanes.
These streets where generations
lived lives. Shared looks. Our speech.
Come in, wee weans
Come yous in for sweets
An' we'll go'er the shore a dander.

My aunts in their pinnies
are at their doorstep greeting,
the smell of baked cake drifts
from the kitchen. Here is home
to chiming clocks, old photos, china
cups, topped-up holy water fonts.

In Montgomery Terrace behind lace curtains
between Holy Hours, Benedictions
they have hushed conversations
intent in their talking
and in their listening
I know rightly, aye surely.

Lena, our maiden aunt,
our unclaimed treasure, raised brow
and head nodding at news.
Little setbacks. Surprises.
Strays an eye to the window
as a neighbour passes.

And then their helpless laughter
when Mercedes jokes
(half in earnest)
People unkind to others
should be placed
against a wall and shot.

Heirloom

The thing I asked for
was the egg-timer from the kitchen wall.
It hung motionless amid family babble
between a pincushion and the Sacred Heart.
Unnoticed until turned upside down
the two glass lobes came to life.
A little rush of streaming sand
let time fall.

The place we thought
we'd never leave
now a world away.
Behind us
but not erased.

For here in this digital age
between plasma screen
and grandchild's art, the face
inverted, calibrated still
shows the minutes slide
even as we sit 'mid young
family voices buoyant at the breakfast table.

Summerdale

In another time on Bishop O'Donnell Road
near roundabouts and traffic lights,
built in Rahoon countryside.
Victorian style. Iron railings.
Home to birth, children's laughter.

The Society of Friends built it.
In later times a doctor practised
raised a family here.
Patients came to talk. He listened.
Felt pulses. Tapped backs.
Placed a stethoscope on beating hearts.

For years I've watched
its weathered gates stuck half-open
paint-flaked windows, flimsy curtains
keep light and life out.
I imagine a silent hallway. No patients
no visitors now come to knock.

Binnion Road

Not hedged nor winding.
Straight, tree-lined
it took us from the village
towards the shore.

The trees arched overhead
in summer. We sped on bikes
through speckled tunnels
light-headed, free.

Tinkers camped along grassy verges
stick-smoke wafted as we passed
mysteries of florid caravans
tethered piebalds, the lurcher's stare.

Winter nights our lights explored
wooded life of silent dark. We peered
through trees, listened to the rise
and fall of anxious breath.

Keeping On

i.m. Patricia Kavanagh

Alone, from now on, she surveys
the street. No movement or sign
of those neighbours, good for chatter
about the weather, get her day started.

Useless to think she'll hear my father's
key in the door, his footsteps in the hall
or the noise of the children play catch me
drift down to her from upstairs.

She may take refuge in her piano,
practise arpeggios, with a light touch
play 'The Robin's Return' or 'The Gentle
Maiden' she once taught me for Derry Feis.

Kitchen routines restore her.
Everything just so, pots and kettles
on the range, she plumps dough
waits for bread to bake.

She scans the sky. Clean washing
sways on the line. She sits a while
rises for a thimble, threads a needle
soothed by the pull and catch of stitch.

Gratitude to Rose Bradley, Annabella Comiskey

Had I Not Been Awake I Would Have Missed It

after Seamus Heaney

A hum at first that swelled
to harmony through an open window.
Trumpet, clarinet, trombone,
in trance-like rhythm. New Orleans
adrift in night air over Clifden Square.

A double bass strummed insistent
cardiac beats, cymbals and a drum roll
announced a solo; a man shouted 'Yeah'.
The repeating riff of clarinet

soothed and sweetened by heart-hunger from the brass.
Chants and beating pulses; call and response blues.
A rousing blast preceded the startled stop.
Murmured cheers gave way to street talk
and the night's dying note.

That Name

Bestowed at Baptism
by priestly reverence
for a Pope of Rome,
I never felt
it was my own.
It lacked
a sporting-hero ring.
I knew
no breathless girl
would cling
and whisper
in my ear
'I love you

Pius'.

Poll an Phíobaire

The Piper's Cave
opens at Súil Rock
on the face of Binnion Hill.
No one knows how far in it goes.

Long ago a piper entered
the empty chamber and played
to find out. His friends above ground
listened to hear the direction he was taking.

The tune he was playing was:

'Béidh na cailíní óga ina seanmhná
        'The young girls will be old women
Sul a bhfille mé, sul a bhfille mé.
        Before I return, before I return.
Béidh na huain óga ina seanchaoraigh
        The young lambs will be old sheep
Nuair a thiocfas mise ar ais.'
        Before I come back again.'

He journeyed the dark alone
shrill echoes of his piping
trapped. Overhead the friends
followed the sound as far as
Lower Annagh where they lost
track. The story the old people had
was that he never came back.

Irish text taken from original recording of Charles McGlinchey by my father,
Patrick Kavanagh, and published posthumously.

Charles McGlinchey, *The Last of the Name*. Edited and introduced by Brian Friel.
Belfast: Blackstaff Press, 1986: 64.

McGlinchey, Charles, Patrick Kavanagh, Desmond Kavanagh, and Nollaig Mac Congáil.
An Fear Deireanach den tSloinneadh. Galway, Ireland: Arlen House, 2002.

The King's Instructions

Seán the Tailor saw a crowd of fairies
riding on horseback through a field.
They called to him:
'Come with us to Scotland. Jump
on a white calf.' Their king warned Seán
not to speak until they were home.

They set off and toured Scotland.
Back across the Moyles to Malin they journeyed.
At Cnockamenny Bens, the horses and the calf jumped
over the bar mouth of the Isle of Doagh.
Seán shouted: 'That was a great jump for a calf'
Horses and fairies and calf disappeared.

He was left alone, down around Lagahurry.
When he got home, it was milking time next forenoon.

Poem based on story as told by Charles McGlinchey and recorded by my father,
Patrick Kavanagh. See page 23.

Pilgrimage to the Breeders' Cup

for John Mac

At Shannon Airport en route to Kentucky,
we see young US soldiers in fatigues
swarm the lounge. Time for most
on their side for now. Yet,
any day soon, others may get
their final boarding call.
Delta flies us west across the ocean
above a sea of clouds.

Amid the hurly burly at JFK,
moving walkways transpose
suited businessmen with briefcases
upright and long lined.
They glide along
like people from another time.

At Cincinnati Red supporters
on mint juleps celebrate
a big baseball win.
We enjoyed the commotion
until our flight was called.
Like the resurrected, we soon were raised again.

Jet-lagged over Lexington
we see an empty Keeneland Racetrack
where tomorrow vast crowds will come
to see great thoroughbreds run.

By now, landed in Syria or Baghdad
the Shannon soldiers wait.

They're Off

Rough diamonds and chancers,
new tipsters, big punters,
swarm around bookies
collecting winnings.

The last race was easy
the easiest race ever. Young lads
in tight jackets won bundles of money.

In the marquees
it's heels, high fashion.
Not here for horses
best dressed the winner.

The next race is a handicap
the trickiest ever. A benefit
for the bookies – best go for a drink.

The bar's now a gaggle of winners
and losers, everything to play for
like horses that jigjog at the start.

The big race is the Group race
the best race ever.
Look, the runners are off.

The crowd crane forward.
The jockeys crouch low.
'Gwan Gwan' shout men in flat caps.

The stands come alive
thrill to the thunder
of hearts and hooves pounding.

The horses fly by, neck and neck.
Here comes the result and…
the favourite's the winner.

That Voice

He looks up from his play-bricks:
'Mary, why do you use that voice
when you speak to me?'
He's all of four.

'Tom, why do you use that voice
when you speak to me?'
'Because it's my voice, you see'.
Here is something to hold on to
until he gets bigger, wiser, older.

But he did and now
he's a rower
a swimmer
a debater
a drummer
who plays keyboards well
into the night.
That voice
a basso profundo.

This May Morning

I stop to watch
the Shannon to New York
Aer Lingus jet rise
over the haze on Clare hills
beyond the lighthouse.
It noses on north-westwards
ever higher
like a wild kite
in the summer sky,
its wake
a disintegrating feather.

Gulls flock and squawk
on a low tide,
the shoreline recedes from
our spread-out town.
Traffic inches
across its linear face.
The day settles in homes, schools,
colleges, industrial estates.

I imagine the 747
by now, a speck
somewhere up there
over the ocean.

I Beg You to Take My Child

A mother's letter to the NY Foundling Asylum 1870's

Kind sisters, you will find my little boy,
one month old tomorrow. His father's gone
and has not been to see him yet.
I work to keep three others. His name
is Walter Cooper, not christened,
could you do it? I would not like
him to die without it. I might claim
him some day but now have not a dollar.
Please keep him four months
and if he is not claimed by then,
I cannot yet support him.
I may send him money some day.
Do not forget his name:
Walter Cooper, Walter Cooper.

Before Cinemascope and 3D

at the pictures in the parish hall.
No tip-up seats, no popcorn,
but shared fags lit the dark
when Jack's searching torch had passed.
Dancers glided here on Sunday nights.
We were a separate league:
transfixed by screen spells
the projector's dusty beam.

The serial was our thing.
Could Tarzan, glistening in his loin-cloth
survive? Chained to the cage wall
escape the lion's clutches?
One Thursday night a beast broke free
flew at him, borne
on our anguished cries.

Willie Doherty fled the front row
charged down the aisle:
'get out or he'll eat us alive'.

We too broke free,
stamping and cheering
safe from celluloid terrors
on the big screen.

Awakening

i.m. Patrick H. Kavanagh

In March, daffodils brightened rocky ground
flushed with pale bluebells in harsh soil
on that sloping bank where you put bulbs down
to proclaim spring for us in Donegal.

Again, I enter the garden to see
us there. You stop to consider
new shoots pushing through dark seams
then dig and slice, neat furrows, drills.

I keep my distance but long
to break up the new-turned clay
with a seaside spade. 'Stones give
drainage and hold heat', you'd say
if I were to throw cock-shots
to startle robins. You'd watch
if I wandered off to marshy ground
to splash and seek frog spawn in bull-rushed ponds.

Now, street shouts from children ring out. See here –
that bank lay half forgotten all year, like
life's cycle – yet, I watch
another generation play,
daffodils reappear, memory stays.

Blinking

A person who blinked a heifer
put the evil eye on her
begrudging the owner.

But a red ribbon on a cow
kept that evil eye away, brought
luck, banished misfortune.
So it was no surprise when
half the cattle at Ballyliffin Fair
had a red ribbon tied about them.

Poem based on story told by Charles McGlinchey. See page 23.

Hitting a Golf Ball and Writing a Poem

Inside your head there is time.
Be disciplined in your observation.

Avoid distraction as you
survey the fairway, note undulations.

Have an image but think
stillness, as you build rhythm.

Even the birds should stop singing
at the top of your backswing.

Follow through the hit, the soaring orbit.
Conjure in the mind a fluent finish.

First Visit

Boys crowded the college walks when I saw
them at the gate: my parents in their Sunday
best, hands held for me to shake.

In the visitors' room, we sat on chairs stiff-
backed, pristine sheen under stained glass
windows, an odour of polish off the floor.

Banter from boys echoed along terrazzo
corridors. Scales practice played out while
we talked across the space between us

learning to let go. News of neighbours
unfolded as the bell for study rang out
marking our separation. Parried in small talk

not practised in our leaving, I watched them
linked, closer than I had ever seen them,
head away for home down Bishop Street.

Click

Though you do not smile
the *joie de vivre* of your young lives
beams across a departure platform
at Burgess Hill Station.

So smart in blue casual chic
- twins in doubling attire -
your tranquil gaze so trustful
of your dad, who clicks
and sees himself in you.

From early climbing from your cots
to nimble steps and runs
that presaged athletic bent
you've reached this point, recorded
by an instant reflection of light.
Soon your trajectories will move.

I hear your banter echo down the line.
For now your lives are intertwined;
Karate across the kitchen floor
Lego-kings, *X-Box*, *Spiderman cake*.
Plans to score in Anfield, Croke Park.
Your after-school homework routines.

In time, you'll stand apart, slip
into your own beings, click
with others, come back, feet taller,
bearing those familiar looks
of earlier generations, laugh
at my old jokes.

Malin
Head

Glashedy
Island

DOAGH
ISLE

Malin

Culdaff

Tullagh
Bay

Dunaff
Head

Binnion

Fanad
Head

Dunaff

Ballyliffin

Sraid

Leenan

Clonmany

Carndonagh

GAP OF MAMORE

Dunaff
Bay

Magheramore

Portsalon

Bulaba

Meendoran

Dunree
Head

Mintiaghs
(Meentiagh)
Lough

Lough
Doo

Slieve Snaght
(Sliabh Sneachta)

Lough Swilly

Buncrana

Ramelton

INISHOWEN
PENINSULA

FANAD
PENINSULA

Moville

Rathmullan

Lough Foyle

INCH
ISLAND

DERRY

Far and Near

I drive up Fanad Way
along the Swilly shore
past rocky downslopes
and strands that reflect
the coast of Inishowen.

Past Rathmullan, Portsalon
how close
this headland takes me.
Bending at Fanad Head,
across the bay, I see
lights in houses
that I know, familiar
townlands skewed.
Sheep are white dots
on the Gap of Mamore,
Leenan has its back to the shore.

This is how people here
have always seen us.
I am both far and near
alienated in a place
I thought familiar.
My mother waiting
on the other side.

Uplift

i.m. Pat twin McNamara

Their load lightened at the church door
when they heard the traditional air.
No longer feeling such grave weight
gave ease to their leave-taking.

Paired in perfect timing
they bore him high up the aisle.
Shouldering his coffin
knowing what was fitting

for someone who once stood
in late night company unannounced
to render on flute or in song
'An Chúileann' or 'The Rocks of Bawn'.

On the phone with lines by
Heaney or Kavanagh he remembered
other times he'd call just to say:
'isn't this a lovely day?'.

Westwards from Sligo, his funeral
moved on. At Achill Sound, mist
descended; a great blind drawn across
the horizon. The airs, the lines play on.

Descent

Great white clouds spread
beneath a clear sky.
We fly in the hush
of a jet descending.

Away on the horizon
all is evening-glow and sea-glisten.
We look out together. Enchanted.
Could eternity be like this?

As the flight path lowers
we are carried through
an interplay of blue and mist, discern
a great patchwork of fields

bisected by a never ending dual carriageway.
Sailing boats on the Solent, trim edge
of England's coast, the Isle of Wight
where we will be hosted.

Bournemouth Airport looms ahead
its runway rises to meet us.
Two souls, in the out-of-world
splendour of a sun-drenched Dorset evening.

Election Art

after Philip Larkin

Vote for me
choir solo politicians
from pole positions.
Passers-by see
studied styles, friendly smiles
framed in harbours, sunny skies
poles apart, in rows together.

By night new image makers
change the art
with schoolboy markers.
Posed shoots acquire free glasses
gapped teeth beneath moustaches,
a lady with a pipe lit,
exaggerated private bits.

Tribal Naming

Desmond: my parents felt
Each name should have importance.
Solidarity with precedent
Memory an instinct they followed.
Overcame saintly offers
Not sought that arrived, guaranteed
Delivery from holy orders

Kavanagh, a South of Ireland clan
And Desmond meaning South Munster
Vouch for their intent, call to mind
Ancestors of our name who travelled
North to back Chief Hugh O'Neill
And stayed. Begat our breed
Guardians from that time
Hallowed by the name.

Vicarage Garden Party in Its Finest Hour

A nation of gardeners wends its way
down Sloane Street in May
to Chelsea hoping to be inspired with new plans
for urban lawns, allotments, in home places
like Gillingham, Altrincham, Rye.

Chelsea Pensioners parade in red tunics.
Pleat-skirted women admire flower beds
in flocks: Magnolia, Paeony, Phlox,
drawn to the unusual and scented.
Men in straw boaters and blazers, with Pimm's
check cold frames, greenhouses, sheds.

Near David Austin's Rose Gardens
a brass band goes oompah
a chorus of song fills the air
crowds stand, heads high
hands clasp chests.

There'll always be an England.

Victorian Armchair

I stand my ground so folk may sit
alone in thought or find a voice
with other seated friends in talk.

These hundred and fifty years
I've moved around; manor house
or suburban pile suits best.

In auction rooms I've known the need
to be possessed, Bonhams of Bond Street
the last time I sat that waiting test.

Many admire my broad-winged back
these ball and claw mahogany feet
such upper-class chic.

A daily sitter is the lady of this house
who some days stays to read a book
and tucks her playful grandchild in.

Big-girthed frames seek support
my contours draw them here. They sink
their buttocks into this velvet lap.

I've felt the heat of red-faced squires,
pious parsons, metal merchants, prosperous
farmers, late night tipsy drowsers.

If only I could write a book and tell who tarried here:
the quiet, the snuggled lovers,
good yarn spinners, the odd cranky bastard.

Love Observed

You savour summer
on this coral strand.

Striped towels laid out near
Mediterranean's ebb and flow.

Your red bikini, poppy bright
spotted on a shopping trip.

Black lustrous hair swept back
ponytail at your neck.

Light-headed, I look down
from a balcony. Unseen.

I have no wish to be younger, older
or stand elsewhere.

Everything between us
on hold just now.

Together.
Apart.

Full Circle

i.m. Peter McGettigan

You live out the country life
its intimacies and lore.
Bright lights of Dublin, London behind
you settle for Lough Eske's shore.

You roam hedged roads, moorlands
Blue Stacks, with gun and red setter
or with conditions right
you'd fly-fish the lake.

In city life your comic-turns
were legend. Hunkered down you mimed
a duck shoot in the Toby Jug,
Bunch of Grapes, at Ascot Races.

Past Ben Bulben heading North
the road straightens
at Mullaghmore, the sea
comes into view, spirits lift,
you are ahead, expectation
perched on the high stool.

As we walk into The Central,
your listening post and sounding plate
as usual you are yarning,
scrutinise the crowd as you turn
with a big smile when you see us.

Daily, people who never left,
greet you in accents you once missed.
In their easy conversations
say they're glad to see you back.

Galway Air Ambulance

I am grounded in potato drills, flower beds;
above sycamores, at the garden's end,
a helicopter descends. Lights flash
on the underside and at the tail,
a single propeller blade whirs overhead.
I imagine a lone patient, in some distress,
poor soul, the journey a revelation.
Medical help on hand and resuscitation gear.
Ahead, the cardiac team gloved and gowned
have studied an electrocardiogram sent
in recent minutes by a referring hospital
in Connaught, Longford, Donegal.
Time is of the essence.

I am grateful to be here.

St. Patrick's Day

Dum diddlyidle dum, deedledum a day?
                    Deedledum a
                            diddledum, a
                                    doodledum
yeah?
Dal doodle doodle dum
a lum a dum a day.
Lam a lam a dum a dum
diddley aye a doodle dum
diddly aye day! Riddley adley
dum a do... dum a do–
heigh!
Fall doodle (fiddle doodle) lam a dum
a day, diddleyidle doodle dum,
diddleyidle doodle dum, diddleyidle doodle dum......

                                            Day!

Biographical note

Des Kavanagh is a native of Clonmany, Inishowen and lives in Galway. He was educated in St. Columb's College in Derry, University College Galway, and University College Dublin. In London he did postgraduate studies in dentistry and trained as an orthodontist. Since putting down the drill he has taken up the quill.

He has always had an interest and involvement in the arts. Des was co-founder and chairperson of the McGlinchey Summer School in his home place for many years. Through his association with the Clifden Arts Festival, he devised 'Reading and Singing in The Bookies'. Each year, with actor and poet Pete Mullineaux, he co-presents an evening of poems, songs, and stories about horses, ponies, and greyhounds, in Paddy Power's bookies in Clifden.

His work has been shortlisted in the Cúirt New Writing Competition, the Fish Poetry Competition, and Hennessy New Irish Writing in the *Irish Times*, and he has broadcasted on *Sunday Miscellany* on RTÉ Radio 1.

Acknowledgements

Thanks to Mary Ruddy and Vincent Murphy of Artisan House for the loving care and skill they have exercised in producing this collection.

My first tutor was Kevin Higgins at Galway Arts Centre in the company of a very jolly group of learner poets. Thanks to Kevin and the class.

Since then I have been helped by a number of poets.

Notably Mary-Jane Holmes, who has helped me develop my technique and who was chief editor of this collection and decided the order of presentation.

My thanks also to Eileen Casey, who has also been most helpful in directing my development.
Geraldine Mills was another valuable mentor.
I am grateful too to Stan Carey, who did the final edit.

I wish to thank Seamus Deane for his encouragement to publish, and most especially for writing his generous foreword to this collection. He gave it to me just a few months before his death. I thank him also for a lifetime's friendship and influence.

Thanks also to Denis Doherty of Clonmany for the Binnion Road cover photograph, and to Joe Boske for his inimitable artwork. I am grateful for secretarial assistance received in our dental practice, especially from Danielle Furey.

Thanks to my sons, Ronan Kavanagh, for his photograph of Tom, and Conal Kavanagh for his photograph of Ryan, Callum, and Charlie, my four grandsons.

My family have been very encouraging and supportive and kept me going, and for this I thank them.

Acknowledgements are due to the editors of the following publications in which a number of these poems originally appeared: *The Clifden Anthology*, *THE SHOp*, *Skylight 47*, *Lady Gregory's Townhouse*, *Behind the Masks*, *Mosaic*, *Abridged*, and *North West Words*.

Published in Ireland 2021 by Artisan House Ltd.,
Letterfrack, Connemara, Co Galway, H91 N8PK, Ireland.

Editorial Director   **Mary Ruddy**
Creative Director   **Vincent Murphy**
Copy Editor   **Stan Carey**
Illustrations   **Joe Boske**
Printing   **Imago**

Design © Artisan House Publishing, Connemara 2021
Illustrations © Joe Boske 2021 pages 32, 40
Photos © Ronan Kavanagh 2021 pages 28, 53
Photo © Conal Kavanagh 2021 page 38
Cover photo © Des Doherty 2021

ISBN **978 1 9124650 9 5**

A CIP catalogue record for this book is available
from the British Library.

Paper used in the production of this title is made from
wood grown in sustainable forests.

Books of *taste*, Created with *passion*, In the heart of *Connemara*.

Artisan House is a publishing company creating beautifully illustrated
high-quality books and bespoke publications on a richly diverse range
of subjects including food and lifestyle, photography, and the visual arts,
music, and poetry.

www.artisanhouse.ie